NATURAL NEW ZEALAND

D0121143

NATURAL NEW ZEALAND
AN ILLUSTRATED GUIDE

TEXT AND ILLUSTRATIONS BY
DON STAFFORD

REED

Also by the author:

Introducing Maori Culture
Landmarks of Te Arawa — Volume I
Landmarks of Te Arawa — Volume II
Nga Toa Kohatu (Rock Warriors)
Pakiwaitara — Te Arawa stories from Rotorua Rock Warriors
Tangata Whenua: World of the Maori
Te Arawa: A history of the Arawa people

Reed Publishing
Te Karuhi tā tāpui o Reed (Aotearoa) (NZ) Ltd

Established in 1907, Reed is New Zealand's largest
book publisher, with over 300 titles in print.

For details on all these books visit our website:
www.reed.co.nz

Published by Reed Books, a division of Reed Publishing (NZ) Ltd,
39 Rawene Rd, Birkenhead, Auckland 10.
Associated companies, branches and representatives
throughout the world.

National Library of New Zealand Cataloguing-in-Publication Data
Stafford, D. M. (Donald Murray), 1927-
Natural New Zealand : an illustrated guide / text and illustrations by
Don Stafford.
ISBN 0-7900-0914-5
1. Natural history—New Zealand. 2. New Zealand—Description and travel.
I. Title.
919.3—dc 21

© 2003 Don Stafford — text and illustrations
The author asserts his moral rights in the work.

ISBN 0 7900 0914 5
First published 2003

Edited by Carolyn Lagahetau
Typeset by Glenda Rodrigues
Cover designed by Steve Russell

Printed in New Zealand

Contents

Introduction   7

The land before humans   9

Ancestors and survivors   11

    Ammonites   16

    Extinct birds   18

    Survivors   21

Peopling New Zealand   25

    First arrivals   25

    Early plundering   30

    A whalers' port   33

    Gold rushes   36

Notable plants   39

    Nikau   42

    Cabbage tree, or ti-kouka   43

    Pohutukawa   44

    Whau   45

    Kauri   46

    A redwood grove   48

    Flax, or harakeke   51

Some rare land birds   53

    Kiwi   53

    Kakapo   55

    Kea   56

    Black robin   57

    Takahe   59

Special seabirds 61

   Penguins 63

   Australasian gannet 65

   Northern royal albatross 67

Water life wonders 69

   Eels 69

   Giant squid 71

Fishing for dinner 73

Myths, mariners and mountains 76

   Cape Reinga 76

   Kaipara Harbour 80

   City of volcanoes 84

   Waikato River 86

   Mount Egmont/Taranaki 90

   Mount Hikurangi 93

The fire within 95

   The 'thermal wonderland' 95

   Mount Tarawera 98

   The Pink and White Terraces 101

   Lake Taupo 103

   White Island 105

Rock, ice and water 107

   Waikoropupu Springs 107

   Glaciers 109

   Aoraki/Mount Cook 112

   Punakaiki Rocks 115

   Moeraki Boulders 117

   Milford Sound and Mitre Peak 119

Introduction

We would each need several lifetimes to learn something of all the remarkable things that make New Zealand such a special place.

We don't have that opportunity here, but there are many wonderful places we can easily visit and astounding things we can learn if we have some guidance. This little book will provide that.

The author has at some time visited almost every corner of the country and is an acknowledged authority on much of its history and people.

The land
before humans

Two hundred million years ago, New Zealand as we know it did not exist. It was then just part of a vast single southern continent that stretched from the equator to Antarctica. This great land mass included South America, Africa, India, Australia and Antarctica. It was called Gondwanaland after the Gonds, an ancient tribe of northern India.

Then probably about 150–130 million years ago Gondwanaland began breaking up, allowing the separated

pieces to gradually 'drift' in different directions, through the process of sea floor spreading, ultimately taking up positions in the southern hemisphere that we are familiar with today.

Until some 85–60 million years ago New Zealand was part of a piece that included Australia as well as New Guinea. When it finally separated from that piece it moved to the east and a little south of Australia.

However, to begin with New Zealand looked nothing like the country as we know it today. We're not sure exactly what it did look like but we do know that at the time of its separation from Australia it probably extended far enough north to include what is now New Caledonia. Then dramatic rises and falls in sea level (due to climatic changes) at times drowned much of our low lying country, leaving a considerably smaller land area than we know today. Perhaps what was left even resembled an archipelago.

At other times it rose again from the sea and gigantic earth movements heaved and twisted the land, leaving spectacular mountains and alpine chains.

Volcanic activity has similarly and devastatingly changed parts of our landform again and again. Even today it clearly indicates to New Zealanders its remaining and only just suppressed power.

Ancestors and survivors

Although it is 150 million years since New Zealand was part of Gondwanaland we still discover, every now and again, the remains of creatures both great and small that are an inheritance from that remote era.

They are fossil remains, preserved largely in various sedimentary rocks both along our coastline and in inland rock deposits that were once seabed but later lifted high and dry by tremendous earth movements. Sometimes these fossil remains are only fragments of some original creature, but comparison with

Flesh-eating theropod.

complete remains in other countries enables us to identify them fairly accurately.

A large range of fossils has been discovered. Some are of creatures that first roamed across our land while we were still attached to Gondwanaland or perhaps to Australia. Some even survived for a time after we were surrounded by ocean.

Others lived in the sea and some flew about, but most disappeared some 65 million years ago — the time when all the world's dinosaurs became extinct.

Pterosaur.

Ocean-dwelling plesiosaur.

There was, however, one of these amazing creatures living in New Zealand much later, about 35 million years ago. It was one of the world's largest ever penguins, almost as tall as a normal man and weighing probably 100 kg (220 lb).

Giant penguin,
Pachydyptes ponderosus.

Ammonites

Most of our knowledge concerning the age and original forms of New Zealand has come from the work of dedicated geologists. Their efforts and those of their worldwide colleagues have led to an international time scale, which sets out the earth's history into a series of eras, each one of which represents an enormous span of time. Fitting New Zealand's emergence into this recognised time scale depends, in part, on a recognition of fossils, which in this country are predominantly of marine form.

Among these are ammonites, a soft-bodied marine animal (cephalopod) like squid or octopus but, unlike those, it lived and developed within an external shell. It was this shell that set ammonites apart from many other hard-shelled molluscs such as limpets and snails.

The ammonite's shell was coiled and chambered, some of the inner chambers being empty or filled with a mineral deposit to act as ballast while moving through the water. The chambers were separated by a wall, each leaving a distinct ridge on the covering shell.

Although ammonites had probably existed for 200 million years, they have been extinct now for some 65 million years. Surviving fossils, however, give proof of an amazing diversity of size, some being little more than 3 or 4 mm ($\frac{1}{8}$ in) across while others reached much greater proportions.

One of the most remarkable ammonite fossils, and certainly one of the world's largest, was recovered from a roadside cutting near Kawhia Harbour on the North Island's west coast. Though only the edge of this fossil was initially visible, it was first

Ammonites

spotted by an amateur geologist. Experts were called in and the work of extracting it from the surrounding rock was initiated.

An explosives expert began the process by blasting it from the surrounding rock before dedicated geologists began the monumental and exacting task of restoring it to its original form. Today it is on display at New Zealand's national museum, Te Papa Tongarewa, in Wellington.

Extinct birds

Not all creatures that lived in New Zealand millions of years ago had disappeared by the time humans arrived. Two of these were quite remarkable. One was a giant eagle, the largest ever known.

It was probably the hokio, an enormous and fearsome bird spoken of in legends by the early Maori people. Remains identify an eagle with a wingspan of some 2.4 m (8 ft), a powerful curved beak and heavy legs with massive claws. It might have weighed as much as 12 kg (26 lb) and certainly could have struck down and killed any of New Zealand's other birds existing at that time. Its weight and speed when diving onto prey would have been sufficient to stun even a fully grown moa, one of the world's mightiest birds.

Artefacts made from bones of the eagle have been found in archaeological sites, clearly establishing its coexistence at least for a time with humans. However, with the gradual destruction of its natural habitat as well as a constant reduction of its natural prey due to human occupation, it is believed the eagle became extinct some 500 years ago.

Its contemporary, the moa, managed to survive for probably another century. It was a giant among birds and its ancestry can be traced back through the ages to Gondwanaland, together with the group of southern hemisphere flightless birds that includes the ostrich, emu and cassowary.

The biggest of the moa species, and one of the largest birds that ever lived, stood 3 m (10 ft) tall and weighed sometimes more than 250 kg (550 lb). Its flightlessness was compensated

Extinct birds

Giant eagle, or hokio.

Extinct birds

for with its powerful legs, ideally suited for running away from a predator or defending itself with slashing kicks.

A browsing plant-eater, the moa was widespread throughout New Zealand during the early period of Maori occupation. It is believed to have been hunted to extinction by these people before the end of the seventeenth century.

Moa, *Dinornis giganteus*.

Survivors

There were other creatures of Gondwanaland origin that, despite a now endangered status, have survived. Remarkably, it is only here in New Zealand that they can be found.

Prominent among these is the tuatara (*Sphenodon* species). Resembling a large lizard, the tuatara is the world's only surviving reptile from an otherwise extinct group akin to the dinosaurs. It grows to perhaps 60 cm (2 ft) in length and weighs around 500 g (1 lb). The tuatara exhibits many primitive features that set it

Tuatara.

Survivors

apart from all other creatures. Strangely, its living quarters are burrows in the ground, which it shares with various seabirds.

Tuatara have the slowest growth rate of any reptile. They mature at around 13 years old and often live over 60 years. Claims are made that they may survive for as long as a century. Found now only on some 20 of New Zealand's smaller islands, they are an endangered species and totally protected by law.

Another much smaller though fearsome-looking resident is the giant weta (*Deinacrida* species), an insect with a background of at least 200 million years. Leading a predominantly nocturnal life, the several species of this amazing animal scramble about our forest floor and into shrubs and trees. When disturbed the weta raises its huge hind legs, which carry a series of extremely sharp spines.

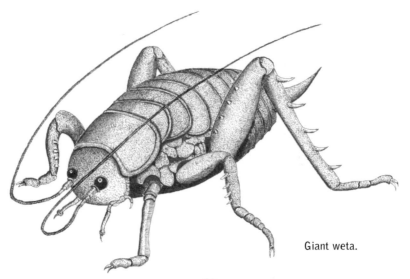

Giant weta.

Survivors

Weighing as much as 70 g (about 2 oz) and with a body length of up to 10 cm (4 in) it is probably the largest insect in the world. Its numbers have been reduced dramatically since the introduction of rodents. Though its main habitat today is on offshore islands, it still survives in some mainland locations.

The New Zealand lesser short-tailed bat (*Mystacina tuberculata*), a remnant of some ancient ancestor, is unique among all bats. Well able to fly, with a wingspan of some 25–30 cm (10–12 in) and a heavy mouse-like body, it is nevertheless the only ground-dwelling member of the bat family. For this reason it has developed specialised and powerful legs allowing it to move comfortably through forest floor debris or

Short-tailed bat, *Mystacina tuberculata*.

Survivors

climb into trees. It also uses its folded wings as 'front limbs' for scrambling around. When not flying, a complicated wing-folding system provides protection for the delicate wing membrane within small pockets at the side of the body.

Distinctive features of this small creature are its pointed ears, large prominent nostrils and a short, stumpy tail.

Together with another bat (a much later New Zealand arrival) the lesser short-tailed bat was the only mammalian inhabitant of this country at the time of initial human occupation. It is now found only at a few scattered sites.

Peopling
New Zealand

First arrivals

The most dramatic event for New Zealand took place some time between AD 700 and AD 1000. It was then that the first humans arrived — Polynesians who after many centuries of migratory voyages from their central Pacific homeland reached these shores.

Speculation and argument still persist over how and when they accomplished their remarkable voyages but accomplish them they did, and they have occupied these southernmost habitable South Pacific islands ever since.

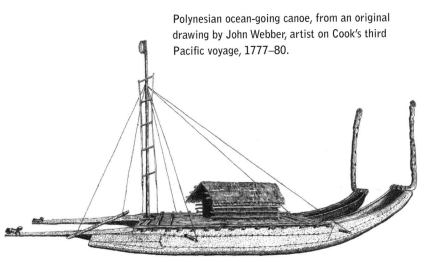

Polynesian ocean-going canoe, from an original drawing by John Webber, artist on Cook's third Pacific voyage, 1777–80.

First arrivals

Though a triumph for the Polynesians, their arrival in Aotearoa (as New Zealand became known to them) was a disaster for the wildlife that existed here at the time. Apart from the two species of bat there were no other land-dwelling mammals and therefore no mammalian predators, which had led to a remarkably diverse birdlife. That same lack of predators had freed the birds from competition on the ground, resulting in many foraging for food on the forest floor or open grassland. In time this led to a reduced need for flight, then a reduction of wing size with a consequential growth of the body.

With the Polynesians came the dog and the rat, which along with hunting and habitat destruction by the new human inhabitants ultimately meant extinction for some 40 percent of those birds breeding in New Zealand when the seafarers first arrived. Most had disappeared before the eighteenth century.

Polynesian dog, or kuri.

First arrivals

History tells us that the first non-Polynesian to reach New Zealand was Abel Tasman, a Dutchman who skirted part of our coastline in 1642. Without landing (although some believe he probably did) he sailed away and another 127 years passed before the next white faces — those sailing with James Cook in the *Endeavour* — reached our shores.

But there may have been others who appeared here, some perhaps more than a century before Tasman.

Maori traditions from Hokianga in the north to Otago in the south retain stories of strangers arriving at some remote period. They speak of white people with muskets appearing in the Hokianga Harbour, and of a similar group being 'cut off' by local tribes in the same area. There are stories of a fishing party off East Cape being approached by a foreign ship manned with white people and of a similar vessel being totally wrecked in the Cook Strait area.

Polynesian rat, or kiore.

27

First arrivals

Legends exist of fair-skinned strangers landing further south who wore shiny coats against which Maori weapons had no effect, and even as far south as Shag Point in Otago local tradition has it that a strange ship brought 'pakeha [foreign] things' to the people there some 500 years ago.

Maps of the world, some produced as early as 1536, are said to include coastline areas of both Australia and New Zealand. The inference is that they were based on information supplied by Spanish or Portuguese ships, both of which were operating in Pacific waters during the early sixteenth century.

A number of unidentified shipwrecks exist around our coasts. Though none has been examined by experts, there are claims that at least two may be relics of Spanish or Portuguese vessels. Support for an early Spanish arrival is generally attributed to a Spanish iron helmet (of circa 1580 vintage) dredged up from Wellington Harbour about a hundred years

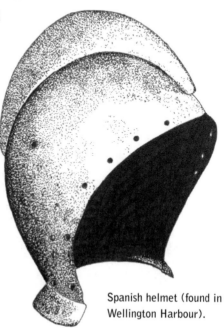

Spanish helmet (found in Wellington Harbour).

First arrivals

ago. Though proving little it has fuelled much speculation.

One of the most remarkable artefacts, however, is a bronze bell recovered in the 1830s from a Maori group near Whangarei, who were using it as a cooking pot. Its owners claimed it had been discovered in the roots of a large tree that had fallen many years before. Cast some time about AD 1450, the bell carried a raised inscription in ancient Tamil (southern Indian) characters identifying it as the bell of a ship belonging to Mohaideen Bakhsh. How such an artefact found its way to New Zealand is a mystery and despite great debate will probably remain so.

Tamil bell.

Early plundering

Less than 30 years after Captain Cook had visited New Zealand and described the incredible wildlife on its shores and in its waters a bloody episode began which still leaves some of those species reeling from its effects.

In 1792 a gang of sealers was left at Dusky Sound to hunt fur seals for their hides, which commanded a high price in China and elsewhere. Other gangs soon arrived and within a year or two the seals were killed in numbers that almost defy imagination. A single ship would expect to take as many as 9000 in three weeks. In that same era 45,000 were known to have been killed by two ships and their combined crews of 60 men. Nothing could withstand such slaughter and by the 1830s fur seals were virtually extinct in the southern oceans.

Fur seal.

Early plundering

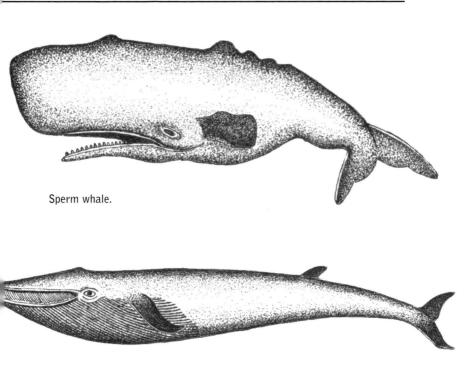

Sperm whale.

Blue whale.

Only now, almost 200 years later, and totally protected by law, are fur seal numbers giving hope of a revival.

With the destruction of the seals attention turned to whales, which in the beginning was a simple operation. Shore stations were set up and the whales intercepted as they followed their ancient migratory routes along the coasts. The killing was intense and when shore stations were no longer worth operating

Early plundering

the great era of pelagic whaling — chasing them across the oceans — began.

No whale was safe from the attention of the hunters and the smaller and slower species were the first to suffer. During the initial 17 years of the nineteenth century almost 200,000 southern right whales alone were slaughtered so that they became almost a rarity.

The final result in those early years was the inevitable destruction of any whale that sailing ships could reach and the almost frenzied determination on the part of whaling interests to hunt down every last one wherever it might be.

Humpback whale.

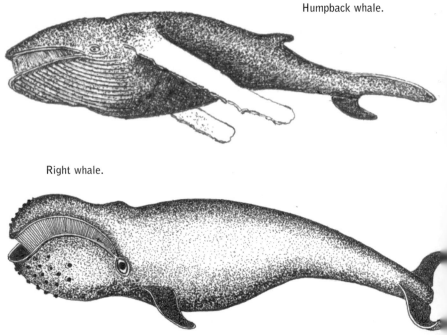

Right whale.

A whalers' port

The whaling industry in particular brought some dramatic changes to New Zealand society. Once news of the rich hunting in its southern waters reached the outside world ships poured in from every corner of the globe. Most came from England, France and America, and the Bay of Islands rapidly became headquarters for those in the trade.

The mid-1830s saw the peak of this first whaling era and Kororareka (now Russell) was by then the major and most notorious of the few European settlements. In 1834 there were 273 American ships alone engaged in whaling — a fleet that employed around 9000 men. The only respite for these crews after sometimes months at sea was their occasional visits to Kororareka for repairs or stores.

In that same year there were 20 grog-shops and probably as many brothels. A writer of the time commented: 'the scenes of immorality and drunkenness ... are truly shocking ... it is not an uncommon sight to see near one hundred sailors roving about Kororareka Beach, most of whom are drunk, and about ten or twelve pitched battles are the inevitable consequence'. The lawlessness and lack of authority soon earned Kororareka the title of 'Hell-hole of the Pacific'.

One strange result of the mix of nationalities gathered together in New Zealand to hunt whales was the commerce that flourished at Kororareka.

In 1838 there were a thousand Europeans living there. It was a settlement composed of sailors, runaway convicts, traders, sawyers, beachcombers, adventurers, settlers, a handful

33

A whalers' port

of missionaries and various government representatives trying
to establish some sort of order.

Though bartering with goods and services was commonplace,
especially when Maori were involved, cash deals were made in

Typical nineteenth century
whaling ship.

A whalers' port

whatever currency was available at the time. As a result the coinage of America, Spain and her colonies, most Latin American republics, France, England and even mintings of the East India Company were all assigned a relative value to English currency and accepted without demur. In fact, up until 1849, long after New Zealand had become an English colony, foreign coinage still circulated and was recognised officially.

American ten dollar gold eagles, Spanish doubloons and silver dollars (pieces-of-eight), French francs, English gold sovereigns and silver crowns and East India Company rupees together with a host of other foreign coins mixed together freely during those early years.

Gold rushes

As well as earlier rushes to New Zealand to gather the riches from our surrounding seas and the mighty northern forests there were other rushes when news of gold being found here reached the outside world.

As early as 1842 whalers had found traces of gold in the Coromandel area but it took another ten years (and the lure of a £500 reward) for a payable alluvial source to be identified. The reward went to Charles Ring, who made the find in September 1852 close to the present Coromandel township. But the find was of little consequence and those who had rushed there were gone within a few months.

Exploration then turned to promising sites in the South Island's northern districts and West Coast. There were some minor rushes but by the end of the 1850s the initial speculation and enthusiasm had waned.

Then in May 1861 an Australian prospector, Gabriel Read, discovered a rich source of gold at Tuapeka in Otago. Within three months some

Gold rushes

2000 hopefuls had joined him and by August there were another 4000 nearby at Waitahuna. Between July and December of that year Otago's population rose from 12,000 to over 30,000, more than half the increase coming from Australia.

In response to the offer of a reward for the discovery of a new field, two Californians, Hartley and Reilly, set out in 1862 and

Gold rushes

made a rich find on the Clutha River near Cromwell. By August they had recovered over 1000 oz (28 kg) of gold, sparking a rush that brought some 3000 new prospectors there within a month. Hartley and Reilly were promised the reward provided 16,000 oz (454 kg) of gold was recovered within three months. In fact, by year's end over 70,000 oz (1980 kg) was lodged in Dunedin, not counting what miners had carried out themselves. It is claimed one prospector once washed out 200 oz (6 kg) of gold with a single dish!

Late in 1862 there were more rich finds. The first were in the Wakatipu area on the Arrow, Shotover and Cardrona rivers, which attracted more than 6000 diggers within a month. Then during May 1863 the Taieri and Manuherikia rivers were targeted, bringing another 2000 men to work near Naseby.

The enthusiasm for prospecting then moved once more to the Nelson and Marlborough districts as well as the West Coast. In March 1865 Westland was proclaimed a goldfield and the town of Hokitika was established. During that same month some 4000 miners arrived and by April there were 7000, many of them coming from Australia. It was called the 'Australia Invasion' and led to a population of 16,000 by September.

Then began the great era of sluicing, dredging and quartz mining, which has provided an industry in both islands for more than another century.

Notable plants

By the time humans arrived in New Zealand, perhaps 1000 years ago, the land was heavily forested. Some 78 percent of the land area was covered, the principal tree species being podocarps (conifers) having an almost unmodified ancestry of at least 190 million years back to Gondwanaland. Apart from having one of the world's largest of this species, the kauri, New Zealand also has the world's smallest — pigmy pine (*Dacrydium laxifolium*). When mature, pigmy pine may reach a mere 1 m (39 in) in height; some pigmy pine only 75 mm (3 in) tall have been known to form fruit.

Though 'the bush' (as most New Zealanders refer to our native forests) possesses an amazing range of species, it presents a somewhat gloomy aspect, the dull green and leathery textured foliage of the almost totally evergreen flora being the reason. There are less than a dozen native deciduous species to be found.

There are, of course, exceptions and apart from the numerous flowering shrubs there could be few more beautiful sights than the summer scarlet blossoms that cover our coastal pohutukawa (*Metrosideros excelsa*) and its near relative the forest rata (*Metrosideros robusta*) or the early spring-blossoming kowhai (*Sophora* species) with its rich golden blossoms.

Tree ferns.

New Zealand also possesses an amazingly rich diversity of ferns, often earning it the title of 'The Land of Ferns'. The silver tree fern frond has, in fact, become almost a national emblem.

Ranging in size from giant tree ferns to a multitude of small and delicate forest-floor species, the ferns, together with flowering shrubs, represent a collection of which 84 percent are found nowhere else in the world.

Similarly, this country's alpine vegetation (one of the richest in the world) provides the Southern Alps in particular with a variety of species that are 94 percent unique to New Zealand.

With hindsight we can mourn the loss of so much of our indigenous forests. Fires lit (by design or accident) by our first human inhabitants, Maori, along with fires that occurred naturally, meant the forest cover was reduced from 78 to about 53 percent by the time Europeans first settled here. In the less than 200 years since then our native forests have been reduced again, this time to about 25 percent of their original extent.

Nikau

Found in many coastal, lowland and hilly forest areas of New Zealand, this genus consists of three species, one of each being located in the Kermadec Islands, Norfolk Island and New Zealand. The New Zealand species (*Rhopalostylis sapida*) has the distinction of being the southernmost naturally occurring palm in the world, adding an almost tropical appearance to some parts of our otherwise temperate zone forests.

In areas where nikau were abundant the palm was utilised as thatch for general housing and very often as temporary shelter for those involved in forestry work up until the early years of the twentieth century.

Cabbage tree, or ti-kouka

Common throughout New Zealand, particularly on cleared swampy land, cabbage trees (*Cordyline australis*) with age can attain a height of 20 m (65 ft) with massive trunk and head. The fleshy inner root and tender palm heads were once a valued food source for Maori, while the leaves provided a strong and suitable material for a variety of woven and plaited products. Early European settlers also made good use of these trees. The hollowed out trunks (which would not catch fire) were often used as chimneys for their original dwellings. They too cooked and ate the palm-head hearts, which were said to taste like cabbage, hence the name cabbage tree. Until recently the cabbage tree was classified as belonging to the family Liliaceae, providing it with the title of the world's largest lily. Though still closely related to the lily, it is now included among the Agavaceae and may well now be the largest of all agave.

Pohutukawa

Pohutukawa (*Metrosideros excelsa*) belongs to the family Myrtaceae, which includes 100 genera and some 3000 species. They range widely throughout the southern hemisphere and particularly across the South Pacific latitudes.

The five New Zealand *Metrosideros* species are endemic to this country and are regarded with special affection by most New Zealanders, not only for their magnificent display of brilliantly red blossoms but because this phase heralds in summer.

One particular pohutukawa, growing at Te Araroa on the North Island's east coast and named Te Wahoa Rerekohu, is claimed to be one of the world's largest specimens with a height of nearly 20 m (65 ft) and a total spread of over 38 m (almost 126 ft).

Whau

Though belonging to the family Tiliceae, which is found in both tropical and temperate zones, the New Zealand endemic and sole genus, *Entelea*, is a small but particularly attractive tree. Attaining a height of up to 6 m (20 ft), whau (*Entelea arborescens*) also grows as a shrub and is usually covered with pale-green leaves that commonly are 15–20 cm (6–8 in) long and almost as wide. It also produces clusters of largish white flowers and distinctive spine-covered seed capsules unique to New Zealand trees.

The most remarkable feature of the whau is the weight of its wood — about half that of similarly sized cork, it may be the world's lightest. Whau was used by early Maori as floats for their fishing nets, which at times were of great length.

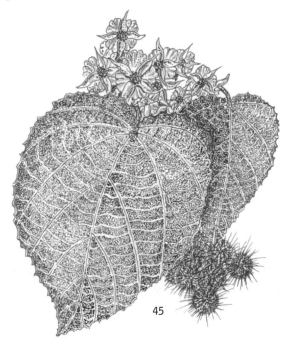

45

Kauri

The whaling fleet, the British navy, boat-builders and traders from all over the world found another rich source to exploit in New Zealand that lasted for the best part of 100 years. When they had finished, New Zealanders themselves continued to strip what was left standing. It was a forest of one of the largest and most majestic trees in the world, the kauri (*Agathis australis*).

Its superb timbers, especially for boat-building, were first recognised in the late eighteenth century. By 1900 over 1.2 million ha (2,900,000 acres) of these forests had been reduced to less than 200,000 ha (494,000 acres). Millions of trees were felled and a great many more simply burnt during a frenzy to satisfy the export trade and clear the land for farming. Even after 1900 the carnage continued, leaving the country today with a mere 7500 ha (18,533 acres) of unmodified mature kauri forest.

It is still possible to appreciate the magnificence of the kauri within the Waipoua kauri forest and several smaller reserves in the northern part of New Zealand. Nothing could have more grandeur than these mighty trees. Most today average 30 m (100 ft) in height with an 18 m (60 ft) clear trunk to the first branch and a diameter of almost 10 m (32 ft). There are, of course, many trees in these forests of much larger dimensions. The largest kauri on record had a girth of 23.43 m (77 ft) and a branch-free trunk of 21.8 m (72 ft).

The production of kauri timber in New Zealand is now strictly controlled and every effort is made to aid the regeneration of this superb tree. In recent years remnants of kauri forests buried

Kauri

beneath our northern swamplands for as long as 45,000 years have been recovered. Much of the timber, in flawless condition, is being used to produce a remarkable range of highly sought after products.

A redwood grove

Standing on the doorstep of the city of Rotorua is the Whakarewarewa Forest Park, host now to a yearly estimate of almost 200,000 visitors. It is a park that can be fairly claimed as one of the major points of origin for the vast exotic forests that are today established throughout New Zealand.

Concern over the rapid depletion of our native forests led to the establishment of an afforestation programme during the 1880s. A 20 ha (50 acre) nursery at Whakarewarewa began the production of seedlings in 1898 and reached its zenith in 1934, a year in which 22 million seedlings were produced. Since that time the emphasis of the nursery has been changed and refined to a much smaller research nursery, adjacent to the New Zealand Forest Research Institute Ltd.

During 1899 plantings were made of some 170 species of exotic trees from various parts of the world, intended to determine, particularly, the most suitable to be grown on the central North Island volcanic plateau lands. By 1916 the original forest area, except for some patches of native bush, which still exist, was fully planted. Many of these species failed to survive and others proved of little value. However, one in particular, radiata pine, has subsequently become the most important commercial species in New Zealand. Others such as European larch and Douglas fir also provide commercial crops and each adds an element of beauty to an otherwise rather gloomy and often vast landscape.

Though proving unsuited here for large scale forestry development, it is without doubt the 6 ha (15 acre) grove

48

A redwood grove

A redwood grove

of coast redwood (*Sequoia sempervirens*), planted in 1901, that are the most admired trees within all our exotic forest plantations. This particular species, though not yet as tall as its forebears in California, is exquisite in form and creates a tranquil and cathedral-like atmosphere for all who enjoy a stroll or run on the well formed and maintained tracks running throughout the area.

The redwood grove is of particular significance to all New Zealand forest workers as it serves as a memorial to former Forest Service personnel who gave their lives in the two world wars.

Flax, or harakeke

Undoubtedly the most important non-food plant in pre-European New Zealand was the native flax (*Phormium tenax*), known to Maori as harakeke. It forms one of our more distinctive endemic landscape features and is otherwise found only on Norfolk Island, to the northwest of New Zealand.

Flax

A herbaceous plant of the largely southern hemisphere Phormiaceae, it was first described as *Phormium tenax* by the botanists J.R. and G. Forster, who accompanied Captain Cook during his second voyage to New Zealand in 1772. The term is derived from the Greek *hormos*, a basket, and the Latin *tenax*, strong, and alludes to the baskets made from the leaves of the plant by Maori of the time.

A somewhat smaller species, known to Maori as wharariki (*Phormium cookianum*) is generally referred to as mountain flax. This, however, is misleading, as the same plant can be found from sea level to heights of almost 1400 m (4500 ft). Apart from this plant's size it is also distinguished by its flowers, which may vary from orange to yellow.

The distinctive rigid leaves of *Phormium tenax* vary in length from 1 to 3 m (3–9 ft) and up to 12 cm (5 in) across. The woody flower stems, which may reach 4.5 m (15 ft) in height, are extremely light in weight and carry flowers that are invariably of a dull red colour, the generally deep olive-green/black pods producing masses of flattish, glossy black seeds.

More than 60 varieties of native flax were recognised by early Maori and utilised in most facets of their day-to-day lives. The plant also possesses several features that provided products of food and medicinal value.

Fibre extracted from the leaves was much superior to that of the unrelated European linen flax (*Linum usitatissimum*), resulting in an export trade from New Zealand that lasted for more than 100 years to the 1930s.

Some rare land birds

Kiwi

The most noted of New Zealand's flightless birds is the kiwi (*Apteryx* species), a national symbol for New Zealanders today. Of very ancient lineage, this nocturnal forest-dweller possesses a number of unique characteristics.

Kiwi

It has only rudimentary wings and no tail; it has sensory whiskers like a cat, and feathers that give the impression of fur. Unlike any other bird, its external nostrils are at the tip of its long beak, which, together with an acute sense of smell, enables it to probe beneath forest floor debris for its diet of worms, grubs, insects and berries.

Little larger than a domestic hen, the kiwi nests in holes beneath the roots of trees or burrows beneath the ground where the female usually lays one or sometimes two eggs, which she leaves to the male to incubate. Laying one egg is a major accomplishment for the egg generally measures some 13 cm by 8 cm (5 in by 3 in) and weighs about 450 g (1 lb).

Kakapo

One of New Zealand's rarest birds, the kakapo (*Strigops habroptilus*), is in fact the world's heaviest and rarest parrot.

A nocturnal and virtually flightless bird, it is, however, able to climb well and can use its wings for downward gliding over short distances. A solitary dweller, the male bird's courtship efforts include a display area where his performances entail regular low-frequency booms that can be heard up to 5 km (3 miles) away. Like other flightless birds the kakapo has developed a large body that may attain a length of 65 cm (2 ft) and weigh more than 3 kg (7 lb). Kakapo numbers are reduced now to perhaps 50 birds, and a strenuous programme is in place to protect those remaining and encourage breeding.

Kea

Certainly as unique as any New Zealand bird is the kea (*Nestor notabilis*), the world's only true alpine parrot. Native to the South Island's southern region and breeding largely in the Southern Alps, the kea is claimed by some to have a level of intelligence rivalling that of sophisticated monkeys. They have adapted well to the incursion of humans and taken advantage of what they have to offer.

Bold and inquisitive, kea provide much entertainment with their antics and social behaviour. They are also at times destructive, seeming to take a delight in removing with their fearsome beaks and powerful claws whatever can be stripped — such as rubber window seals and shiny radio aerials from parked vehicles.

Black robin

First discovered in 1871, the black robin (*Petroica traversi*) were, even at that time, confined to Mangere Island, one of the remote spots of land making up the Chatham Island group, some 805 km (500 miles) east of New Zealand.

Towards the end of the nineteenth century, depredation due to land clearance, cats and other predators there had wiped out the Mangere Island population, leaving only a smaller, undisturbed group on a nearby windswept, precipitous 7 ha (17 acre) island of rock, known as Little Mangere.

Even here, during the late 1960s, the small remaining colony was reduced drastically when some of its bush area was cleared and a helicopter pad created for the benefit of muttonbird hunters. By 1976 the numbers had been reduced to only seven birds.

Black robin

It was then that a decision was made to transfer this remnant population to Mangere Island, now relatively safe because of a native forest replanting scheme and the demise there of predatory cats. Regardless of this move, by 1980 the robin population had dropped even further to five.

A remarkable wildlife officer, Don Merton, took the task of saving the robins to heart. With his expertise and cooperation from the only remaining breeding pair, a female, Old Blue, and her male partner, Old Yellow, he was able to coax the pair into laying eggs more often than normal. This he did by removing the first clutch and placing them with tomtits on nearby South East Island. There the chicks were incubated, hatched and raised by the tomtits until mature enough to be taken back to Mangere Island and released.

Eventually, robins were also released and established on South East Island as well. Today there is a self-maintaining population of some 150 to 200 of this once nearly extinct bird, their numbers very largely due to the untiring years of dedication given by Don Merton.

A unique feature of the black robin is that they are the world's only wild bird species where the ancestry of each one can be traced back to common ancestors, in this case, Old Blue and Old Yellow.

Takahe

An exciting ornithological discovery was made during November 1948, when a colony of South Island takahe or notornis (*Porphyrio hochstetteri*), thought to have been extinct for at least 50 years, was discovered in a remote glacial valley of the Fiordland National Park, close to Lake Te Anau. Although the species of swamphen had been identified by means of fossil bones as early as 1847, only four live birds were ever noted between that time and the end of the nineteenth century.

Originally two species of takahe lived in New Zealand, with the North Island takahe (*Porphyrio mantelli*), known to Maori as moho, becoming extinct after human occupation. Now the surviving species, in

Takahe

their wild state, are confined to limited areas in the Murchison and Kepler ranges, at altitudes between 762 and 1200 m (2500–4000 ft).

An extremely handsome bird, about the size of a very large domestic fowl, the takahe carries a silky plumage of rich colours including a metallic olive-green back, indigo-blue throat, breast and thigh, and, like its close relative, the pukeko, white under-tail feathers.

Strong legs and feet, and a massive bill, provide the takahe with the ability to tear apart the mountain snowgrass (Danthonia) which, together with seeds and other plant material, provides their major food source. During winter, when snow blankets much of their territory, the birds are able to shelter and forage for food in beech forest that is usually close at hand. Despite fairly large wings, the takahe is flightless.

Soon after the rediscovery of takahe in 1948, their population in the wild was estimated at perhaps 200 pairs. Since that time there has been a gradual decline, with present numbers believed to be around 120 individuals.

However, a brighter future may be ahead. Strenuous efforts are being made to revive the number of this threatened species. A Department of Conservation captive breeding programme at Te Anau has successfully reared several young takahe for release into their natural wild area. A further small number have been introduced to Tiritiri Matangi Island sanctuary, in the Hauraki Gulf near Auckland, where hopes are high for a natural increase in their numbers. Here the birds can be watched wandering about fearlessly, usually within a few metres of visitors.

Special seabirds

There is little doubt that birds were the first and most numerous colonists to arrive in New Zealand after its complete separation from Gondwanaland. Other than ocean mammals, birds alone could cross the great stretches of water under their own power and it was probably seabirds that made those first journeys.

Isolated from any other land mass for perhaps 80 million years and enjoying a total lack of land-based mammalian predators, this country provided a safe haven for the whole range of birdlife that developed here over the centuries.

New Zealand's amazingly long coastline, together with its many offshore islands, has been home to a large and diverse group of seabird species. They range from the graceful albatrosses (*Diomedea* species) with a wingspan ranging up to 2.7 m (9 ft), down to those little migratory marvels, the bar-tailed godwits (*Limosa lapponica*), which fly here from Alaska and Siberia each October/November and return north again during March/April of the following year.

Godwit.

Penguins

Perhaps the strangest of all our coastal birds are the unique penguins. With a greater antiquity than most land-based avians, penguins have evolved in the southern hemisphere and developed the remarkable skill of flying under water rather than in the air.

The most widespread around our coastline is the blue penguin (*Eudyptula minor*), which reaches just 40 cm (15 in) tall and has a bluish tinge to its coat. A solidly built bird, it is often seen on the ocean's surface where it can swim easily or float because of an ability to inflate itself. The smallest of all penguins, it nests ashore, usually in crevices, burrows, the root systems of trees and occasionally beneath seaside houses where its noisy screeching can cause considerable annoyance.

Little blue penguin.

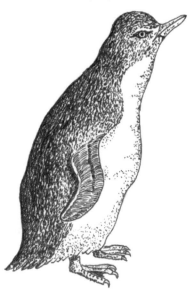

Two of the world's rarest penguins are found around the coastline of the South and Stewart islands. Breeding only in the more remote areas is the Fiordland crested penguin (*Eudyptes pachyrhynchus*), a handsome bird with distinctive yellow crests and heavy bill. Almost twice the size of the blue penguin, it is closely related to the Snares crested penguin of the Snares Islands, part of New Zealand's subantarctic territory.

Penguins

Another uncommon and now endangered bird, the yellow-eyed penguin (*Megadyptes antipodes*) is endemic to New Zealand. It carries a distinctive yellow band of feathers around its head and has a lighter bill than its crested relation. In some restricted areas it can be watched at dusk, swimming in through the surf and hurrying across the beach to the security of nests in the nearby coastal scrub.

Yellow-eyed penguin.

Fiordland crested penguin.

64

Australasian gannet

A magnificent bird in flight, the Australasian gannet (*Morus serrator*), a predominantly white bird with black-tipped flight feathers and golden crown, is commonly seen around the coastline of the North Island and less often further south.

Their spectacular dive into the ocean when feeding, quite often close inshore, is made at a tremendous speed from a height of anything up to 30 m (90 ft). Diving almost vertically, their wings are trailed close to the body just as they enter the water to seize their prey of small fish. In shallow waters their dive angle is less acute. The shock of entering the water is lessened by inflatable air sacs located beneath the skin, covering the breast and lower neck.

Apart from breeding colonies on a number of offshore islands there are three particular mainland colonies that can be viewed at close quarters: Muriwai, on the west coast near Auckland; near the tip of Farewell Spit at the northern extremity of the South Island; and the world-famous Cape Kidnappers colony east of the Hawke's Bay city of Hastings.

The breeding season in New Zealand begins usually in July, with the main egg-laying period occurring between September and November.

Australasian gannet

A single white egg is normally laid in a
depression within a mound consisting mainly
of vegetation, earth and guano. Each nest
is sited just far enough away from the
next to preclude a vicious peck from
a neighbour. Incubation takes
about six weeks, the chicks
arriving black and
naked. They are
soon
covered
with a white
down,
which is
replaced
after about
four months
with a mottled,
greyish brown immature
plumage. By the end of May most

Cape Kidnappers.

young birds have fledged and left the colony,
generally for the eastern seaboard of Australia. Some, however,
travel as far west as the Indian Ocean. Most young New
Zealand gannets remain on the coast of Australia for
somewhere between three and seven years before returning,
generally in their fourth year, to New Zealand to breed.

Northern royal albatross

Nowhere in the world is it possible to visit a mainland albatross colony except at Taiaroa Head, almost part of the city of Dunedin on the east coast of the South Island.

One of the largest of all flying birds, the northern royal albatross (*Diomedea sanfordi*) arrive during September to mate with their lifetime partner and produce a single egg in mid-November. Both parents share the incubation period of about 77 days until the chick hatches in January after a three-day struggle. The task of feeding the chick is shared by both parents and for a start the food consists of regurgitated semi-digested fish fluid. After several weeks the period between feeds is lengthened until it occurs only twice a week. The long sweeps at sea to gather mostly fish and squid for the chick may involve the parent bird travelling

Northern royal albatross

almost 2000 km (1200 miles) in a 24-hour period. Normally their effortless flight allows them a cruising speed of 80–112 kph (50–70 mph), although they have been timed flying at 190 kph (120 mph). Australian researchers have tracked one albatross that in 200 days flew some 50,000 km (31,000 miles).

After 14 weeks the chick is covered with 12 cm (5 in) long down that gradually is replaced with feathers. Then during September, and after considerable practice, the juvenile will launch itself from a cliff and take to the air. From this point on the albatross will spend most of its life (which may well last more than 50 years) very largely at sea, returning to land only to nest.

Water life wonders

Eels

Few countries are as well endowed with water as New Zealand. Streams, rivers, swamps and lakes abound and most are inhabited by eels. Referred to as tuna by Maori, the New Zealand common eel species are the longfin eel (*Anguilla dieffenbachii*) and shortfin eel (*Anguilla australis*). Once taken in prodigious quantities, eels have had their numbers gradually reduced by the ongoing drainage of wetlands, damming of waterways and commercial fishing.

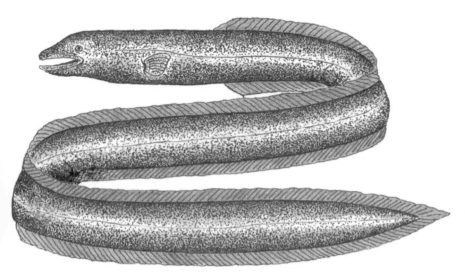

Eels

New Zealand freshwater eels are considered the world's largest. Female longfin eels may reach 2 m (7 ft) and weigh up to 25 kg (55 lb); males may reach only about 70 cm (28 in). The shortfin eel is smaller. The eels of both species most commonly taken, however, would not much exceed 60 cm (2 ft) in length or weigh more than 1–2 kg (2–4 lb).

When fully mature at 20 to 30 years adult eels leave our shores and swim, it is believed, to the tropical waters of Tonga, Tahiti or Fiji where they breed, the female laying millions of eggs. Once hatched, the tiny elvers, perhaps only 5–6 cm (2 in) long, begin their journey of thousands of kilometres back to New Zealand to begin the cycle once more.

Giant squid

New Zealand is one of those rare places in the world where giants of the oceans meet in conflict. One of these is the sperm whale (*Physeter macrocephalus*), sometimes 27 m (90 ft) in length with a great squarish head almost a third the size of its entire body. It is also probably the world's greatest diver, able to descend to depths in excess of 1000 m (3000 ft).

In the waters off the South Island's east coast, between Cook Strait and Kaikoura, the sperm whale spends much of its time. It can usually be seen, especially at Kaikoura, lifting its enormous tail fluke clear of the water to begin its descent into the deep waters, diving to seek one of its favourite foods, the giant squid (*Architeuthis*).

Little of the giant squid is known, except of their size, as occasionally dead specimens are washed ashore, or taken in the nets of deep-sea trawlers. The largest on record was a 20 m (65 ft) individual washed up at Lyall Bay, Wellington, in 1881.

71

Giant squid

In 2002, New Zealand scientists became the first in the world to capture live specimens of the giant squid, although they were unable to keep the juveniles, measuring between 9 and 13 mm long, alive.

Giant squid are the largest invertebrates known and are closely related to octopus and cuttlefish. They are provided with eight muscular arms, each several metres in length and carrying two rows of suckers. There are also two longer and thinner tentacles that, at their extremity, carry a flattened, paddle-like pad, lined with toothed suckers. It is these suckers that seize prey and draw it towards the shorter arms and mouth. Vision for the squid is provided by the largest eyes in the whole animal kingdom, measuring some 25 cm (almost 10 in) in diameter.

Movement of the squid is accomplished by drawing water through a mantle enveloping its body. The intake of water first passes and aerates the large gills, then is expelled forcefully through a narrow funnel that provides a form of jet propulsion, a jet that can be directed to aid manoeuvrability.

Claims exist that giant squid can attain speeds over 20 knots. However, whatever their speed, they and their smaller squid relatives form a major part of a sperm whale's diet. Examinations of the contents of sperm whale stomachs have led experts to estimate that the world's one to two million sperm whales, collectively, consume perhaps a million tonnes of squid each year.

Fishing
for dinner

One of New Zealand's more spectacular and interesting insects is the glow-worm (*Arachnocampa luminosa*). Unique to this country, it is actually a fly, belonging to the gnat family and unrelated to the European glow-worm, which is a beetle. They are found in darker places throughout the country, particularly in abandoned mining tunnels, along shaded stream banks, within damp forested areas and in natural caves.

Where proper conditions exist the female fly will lay as many as 130 tiny spherical eggs, affixing them to some suitable surface from which the emerging larva can suspend its silk 'fishing lines' with which its prey are trapped.

After an incubation period of 20–24 days the tiny worm emerges and immediately begins building a hollow, tubular nest of mucus and fine silk thread, using the same thread to hold it in place against a ceiling or wall. In its larval stage the worm will remain in this nest for some eight to nine months.

The nest, usually some 10 cm (4 in) in length (approximately 2.5 times the length of the larva) can be completed in a surprisingly short time — as little as 10 to 20 minutes. Just as rapidly the larva begins lowering sometimes as many as 70 silk threads, each having a series of sticky mucus droplets at regular intervals, against which smaller insects will become entangled,

hauled up to the nest and consumed. At the same time the larva activates its luminous organ to attract prey and begin feeding.

The remarkable phenomenon of this blue-green light is produced by a chemical reaction involving several components: luciferin (produced in the digestive system), luciferase (an enzyme), andenosine triphosphate, and oxygen.

The light is also activated by the female fly while in her latter pupal stage of some 12–14 days. This attracts the male fly and if successful she will usually mate immediately upon emerging from her pupal case. During the next one to 24 hours she will lay her eggs and usually die almost immediately. Male flies may survive for three or four days.

Most spectacular of all glow-worm sites are at Waitomo, a series of limestone caves that for more than 100 years have attracted an unending stream of visitors. A highlight here is an underground river journey to the Glow-worm Grotto, a vast cavern lit by countless glow-worm lights, rivalling the finest night-time sky.

Myths, mariners
and mountains

Cape Reinga

Standing at Cape Reinga at the northern tip of New Zealand is an amazing experience. Apart from the Three Kings Islands, faintly visible on the horizon, there is nothing but ocean —

Cape Reinga.

Cape Reinga

the vast Pacific that stretches almost another 16,000 km (10,000 miles) north to the Bering Sea.

It is here, also, that another great ocean, the Tasman Sea (lying between Australia and New Zealand), first meets the Pacific, joining with it to create the turbulent waters flowing across the Columbia Bank.

Cape Reinga has always been a place of great consequence to the Maori people. It is there that a wild and rocky promontory known as Te Rerengawairua (The spirits that leap) juts out into the ocean, leading from the highest point (where the lighthouse stands) to a rock platform at sea level some 293 m (961 ft) below. It was to this platform that the spirits of all Maori travelled after death.

Tradition says that after hovering for a time above its abandoned body, the spirit makes a final journey to the high point at Cape Reinga, turns and farewells the land that would soon be lost to view, then descends Te Rerengawairua as far as a lone pohutukawa tree growing on the lower eastern side of the promontory. Exposed roots of the tree reach the rocky platform, enabling the spirit to climb down there for its final moments in this land.

In the sea and close to the platform is a deep hole. As the waves flow in, long masses of floating seaweed obscure the entrance, but, as the water recedes, the hole is fully revealed. It is then that the spirit dives into the hole to begin the long journey to Hawaiki, the mystical homeland and place of origin where the spirit would be reunited with its loved ancestors.

Cape Reinga

Abel Tasman, the first credited European to reach New Zealand, did so on 13 December 1642. On 4 January 1643, his two ships, the *Heemskirck* and the *Zeehaen*, were off the point of land lying a little south and west of Cape Reinga. This he named Cape Maria van Diemen after the wife of the then governor of Batavia. The following day he stood off the group of small islands lying to the northwest. As it was the eve of Epiphany, the day that commemorates the visit of the three wise men of the East to the infant Jesus, he named the group the Three Kings.

Ship of Abel Tasman's time.

Cape Reinga

One hundred and twenty-six years passed before another European ship visited these shores. This time it was the *Endeavour*, commanded by Captain James Cook, who arrived on Friday 6 October 1769.

Travelling slowly up the North Island's east coast, Cook had reached the northernmost point of land (which he named North Cape) by 18 December. His intention was to round it and return south along the west coast. Foul weather, high seas and contrary winds actually took him as far north as the Three Kings, and it was 1 January 1770 before he was back to the west coast.

It is surely remarkable that almost at the same time as Cook was facing the rough east coast seas, Frenchman Jean François

Marie de Surville, in his ship *St Jean Baptiste*, had rounded North Cape from the west and made anchorage in Doubtless Bay, which Cook had named but not entered. Neither was aware of the other, and they were destined never to cross paths.

A nineteenth century engraving of Captain Cook, who first visited New Zealand in 1769.

Kaipara Harbour

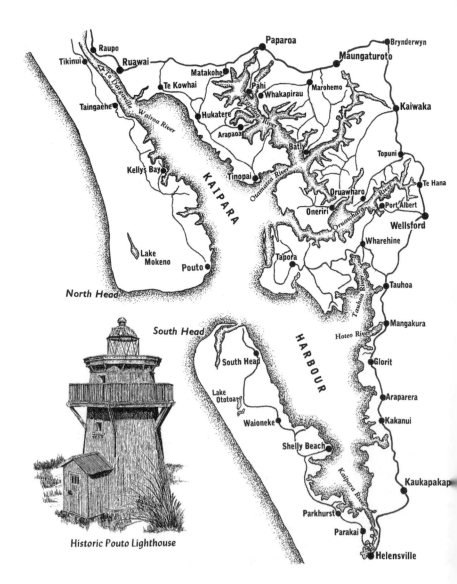

Historic Pouto Lighthouse

Kaipara Harbour

Located some 80 km (50 miles) north of Auckland on the west coast, Kaipara Harbour is the largest of its kind in New Zealand, and, in fact, one of the largest in the southern hemisphere. Its deeply indented coastline, extending over more than 3200 km (almost 2000 miles), once sheltered innumerable settlements as the immense surrounding kauri forests were exploited to a point of almost extinction during the nineteenth century.

Kauri gum and native flax provided other periodic industries, and before the advent of passable roads or rail transport, numerous shipping interests provided regular passenger and freight services throughout the area, stretching from Dargaville in the north to Helensville in the south.

Despite the magnificent ocean coastline and harbour entrance, with its vast, golden sand-hills towering more than 100 m (328 ft) above the sea, the actual entrance (though 7 km wide) has always demanded the utmost caution from navigators entering or leaving the Kaipara. Trapped on the ever-shifting and extensive sand-bars, caught by surging currents, or battered by massive breakers crashing in from the Tasman Sea, more than 100 ships have been wrecked since the first was recorded in 1830.

However, claims are still regularly made that many more unidentified wrecks and other remnants still lie buried outside and within the harbour, or under the Wairoa River's silt, some of which may well pre-date the arrival of Abel Tasman in 1642. These things, together with persistent stories of a pre-Maori population in the area, add an intriguing element.

A lighthouse that operated until 1952 was established at

Kaipara Harbour

Wrybill.

Pouto in 1884. Built solidly of kauri, and casting a 37 km (23 mile) beam, it has withstood the wildest of west coast storms. Ultimately restored and protected by the New Zealand Historic Places Trust, it remains today as almost a lone reminder of the Kaipara's once busy maritime era.

As a comparatively shallow harbour, with innumerable estuaries, extensive mudflats and enormous areas of mangroves, the Kaipara Harbour provides a haven for wildlife, particularly birds.

Some are permanent residents here but the winter months see an influx of others of our native species, most of which are

Kaipara Harbour

normally resident in the South Island. These include pied oystercatchers, pied stilts, gulls, terns, herons, ducks and even occasional visiting godwits, these last remaining here while most of their kind have returned to Siberia. Also among these winter arrivals is the wrybill (*Anarhynchus frontalis*).

Found only in New Zealand, the wrybill is unique among all birds in that the end of its bill curves distinctly to the right, allowing it, with a scythe-like motion, to sweep under rounded rocks as it searches for food.

Together with the Firth of Thames and Manukau Harbour, the Kaipara offers unending scope for wildlife enthusiasts as well as for those with a sense of history.

City of volcanoes

The Bay of Plenty and central North Island area is today generally considered the heart of New Zealand's volcanism. The north to south band of activity, stretching from White Island to Ruapehu, is certainly the country's main active area, and thermal springs, geysers, active volcanoes and the remnants of many dormant or extinct peaks remain along this line. Eruptions from this same chain have probably been going on for some two million years. New Zealand's Tongariro National Park (the world's fourth created national park and the world's first national park to be gifted by an indigenous people) contains three of the North Island's major active volcanoes: Ruapehu, Ngauruhoe and Tongariro.

Further north, another remarkable volcanic area lies largely concealed beneath New Zealand's largest city, Auckland. Within its heavily populated urban area over 40 volcanic cones rise above the surrounding suburbs. Some, fortunately, still hold their original shape, while others have been drastically modified or completely obliterated by quarrying and other commercial activities. The explosion craters of two of these volcanoes are marked today only by inter-tidal basins.

Most of the larger cones also carry clearly defined earthworks, indicating fortifications as well as living and cultivation areas created by early Maori occupants.

This whole volcanic field has seen eruptions for at least 150,000 years, the most recent forming Rangitoto Island some 600 years ago. This event took place well within the period of human occupation, and footprints have been identified beneath a layer of

City of volcanoes

Rangitoto ash. Strangely, no tradition or legend of this event seems to have been preserved by descendants of those original occupants.

Though obviously once an area of intense activity, little seems to disturb the Auckland district today. Earthquakes, for instance, occur less often and with less effect than in most other districts. However, while the whole field now seems to be slumbering peacefully, volcanic activity in the area is still regarded by experts as a potential hazard.

Pupuke

Rangitoto

Tank Farm
(Te Kopuamatakamokamo)

Onepoto

North Head
(Maungauika)

Motukorea

Albert Park
(Horotiu)

Taylor Hill
(Taurere)

Mt. Hobson
(Remuera)

Mt. Eden
(Mangawhau)

Little Rangitoto
(Maungarahiri)

Te Pouhawaiki

Mt. St John
(Te Kopuke)

Mt. Wellington
(Maungarei)

Three Kings
(Te Tatua)

One Tree Hill
(Maungakiekie)

Mt. Roskill
(Puketapapa)

Mt. Smart
(Rarotonga)

Hopua

McLennan Hills
(Te Apunga-o-Tainui)

Puketutu

Waitomokia

Pukeiti

Pukaki

Kohuora

Otuataua

Maungataketake

Manurewa

Matakarua

Volcanoes

of the

Auckland Urban Area

Waikato River

New Zealand's longest river, the Waikato ('Flowing Water'), takes its rise from the snow and ice fields of Tongariro National Park. However, as the various tributaries join they become known as the Tongariro River, which enters Lake Taupo at almost its southernmost point.

The outflow then, from the lake's northeastern point, becomes the Waikato, and from here begins its 354 km (220 mile) journey northwards until finally meeting the Tasman Sea, on the west coast, just south of Auckland.

Though relatively wide for its first 4.8 km (3 miles), the river is then suddenly confined within a narrow, rock-walled chasm, less than 15 m (50 ft) wide and 230 m (250 yards) long. Here it becomes a giant rapid before plunging as a spectacular and massive torrent over a 22 m (73 ft) cliff, known as the Huka ('Foam') Falls. Well-placed viewing facilities make these falls a major visitor attraction of the Taupo district.

Some 8 km (5 miles) below the Huka Falls, the river provides the amazing Aratiatia rapids, created as a result of a drop of some 90 m (300 ft) within a 800 m ($\frac{1}{2}$ mile) stretch of water. Apart from this amazing spectacle, the water here is harnessed to produce electricity, the southernmost of eight hydro-electric generating plants utilising the Waikato River.

Apart from the Aratiatia power station, which is supplied by means of tunnels from a low dam at the head of the rapids, the remaining seven generating plants operate with high dams, behind each of which now lies an artificial lake.

Two further remarkable, but non-hydro generating, plants

Waikato River

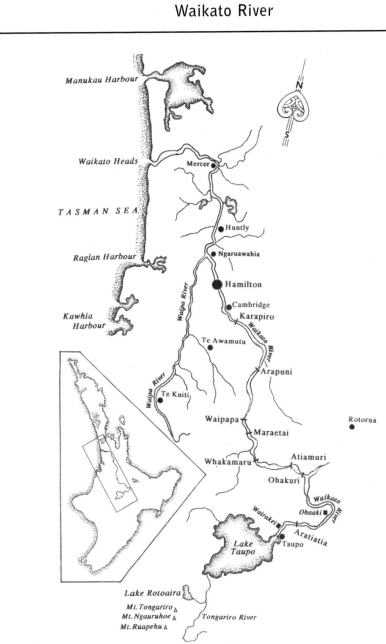

Manukau Harbour

Waikato Heads

Mercer

TASMAN SEA

Huntly

Raglan Harbour

Ngaruawahia

Hamilton

Waipa River

Cambridge

Karapiro

Kawhia
Harbour

Te Awamutu

Waikato River

Arapuni

Waipa River

Rotorua

Te Kuiti

Waipapa

Maraetai

Atiamuri

Whakamaru

Ohakuri

Waikato River

Wairakei

Ohaaki

Aratiatia

Lake
Taupo

Taupo

Lake Rotoaira

Mt.Tongariro △
Mt.Ngauruhoe △   Tongariro River
Mt.Ruapehu △

Waikato River

also utilise water from the Waikato. Their power, however, is drawn as steam from nearby geothermal fields.

Eight kilometres (5 miles) from Taupo is the spectacular Wairakei Valley geothermal field and its nearby riverside power station. Some 25 km (16 miles) further north again, another riverside power station, visible from every direction because of its massive cooling tower, draws its natural steam from the adjacent Ohaaki geothermal field.

For centuries, the Waikato River has provided a form of highway reaching deep into the central North Island. Fleets of canoes once travelled back and forth over much of its length.

Waikato River

Sometimes there were fleets propelled by invading warriors, generally with resulting violent battles against local defenders at almost every bend.

The 1860s even saw military action, when small armoured gunboats travelled up the river to bombard several fortified Maori sites during the New Zealand Wars of that period. The river was also an important access route for early European settlers throughout the area, and commercial vessels regularly plied the waters, a few well into the second half of the twentieth century.

Mount Egmont/Taranaki

New Zealand's most spectacular yet graceful volcano is undoubtedly Mount Taranaki (Egmont/Taranaki is its official name). It enjoys an almost solitary situation on the westernmost bulge of this country's North Island. With its superbly symmetrical slopes, rising to a height of 2518 m (8256 ft), it dominates the surrounding rich farmlands of Taranaki province and is as important to most North Islanders as Mount Fuji is to the people of Japan.

Relatively young geologically, the cone of Taranaki began to form above the older Pouakai and Kaitake ranges (to its northwest) less than 200,000 years ago. Its volcanic history has been marked by periods of violent activity, separated by longer intervals of calm. Its eruptive spasms have spewed lava, huge

Mount Egmont/Taranaki

boulders and a mantle of ash over much of the surrounding countryside.

There is geological evidence that Taranaki may have last erupted as recently as 300 years ago. The discovery in 1929 of an ancient Maori umu (earth oven) beneath undisturbed layers of volcanic ash provides some confirmation of this. Radio-carbon dating of charcoal and scraps of wood from the same oven returned an age of something between AD 1600 and AD 1750. There are also references in Taranaki Maori tradition to an event, perhaps volcanic, which destroyed a village once standing on the slopes of the mountain.

Persistent stories over many years of rumblings from within the mountain, sulphurous smells from time to time, the sighting of steam, claims of hot-water pools and occasional local earthquakes have invited speculation over future volcanic activity. The mountain is certainly regarded by experts as being dormant, but there is little apprehension from those living within sight of it.

Few mountains anywhere have been described in more glowing terms than has Taranaki. They continue today, but those who first saw its elegant form were overawed.

On 12 January 1770, James Cook took his barque *Endeavour* within clear view of the mountain, which he named Egmont '... in honour of the Earl' (the Earl of Egmont, First Lord of the Admiralty). The expedition's famous botanist, Joseph Banks, added his tribute to the mountain, part of which reads: '... how

Mount Egmont/Taranaki

high it may be I do not take upon me to judge but it is certainly the noblist hill I have ever seen …'.

Though the local Maori viewed the mountain with awe and veneration, it served, in places, as a sepulchre for the remains of their dead, rendering the upper slopes extremely tapu. Legend, however, suggests that at least some of their number had in ages past climbed to its highest point. The earliest Europeans to do so were Ernst Dieffenbach and James Heberly who, together, reached the summit in December 1839.

Affection for the mountain and its forested surroundings brought about its creation as a national park in 1900. Of 33,540 ha (130 square miles), the park includes not only the cone of Taranaki but also those of Pouakai and Kaitake, and it serves this country as a favourite climbing and skiing resort area.

Mount Hikurangi

As the sun rises each day its shafts of light strike the summit of Mount Hikurangi on the North Island's east coast. All else lies in darkness. Soon, however, the whole land is bathed in sunlight, the first country in the world to receive such a gift.

Hikurangi, at 1754 m (5754 ft) the highest point in the Raukumara Range, is a sacred mountain to the people whose origins lie in the lands surrounding it. Its importance stretches back well beyond history to a time when Maui, the mythical hero of most Polynesians, was providing us with many of those benefits we take for granted today.

Legend claims it was Maui who gave us Hikurangi and, in fact, the whole North Island of Aotearoa/New Zealand, which was once a gigantic fish that lay deep in the waters of the South Pacific Ocean. While Maui and his brothers fished from their

Mount Hikurangi

canoe Maui hooked this monster and finally dragged it to the surface. Hikurangi was the first part of the fish to emerge and did so directly beneath the canoe; Maui lifted it high into the air. The old people said the canoe of Maui still lay up there on the summit in a petrified state.

Another legend, not unlike the biblical deluge, speaks of a high tide known as Te Tai-o-Ruatapu that once flooded the land. All were drowned except those who had assembled at the very top of that same mountain.

The fire within

The 'thermal wonderland'

From early in the nineteenth century, intrepid adventurers made their way inland to the central North Island to view the area's amazing natural thermal phenomena. Until 1872 there were no roads from the coast, only tracks, pioneered by the original settlers, the Maori, who first arrived here six or seven centuries ago.

Word of the remarkable features to be found in the Rotorua district spread far and wide, and before the end of the century visitors had arrived from every corner of the globe to experience its amazing sights. The flow has never ceased, and few visitors to New Zealand fail to travel here to look with awe (and some times trepidation) on what it has to offer.

The major features of the Rotorua lakes district — its mountains, rocks and lakes — are all volcanic. In geological terms they are also very young, which is in marked contrast to most of New Zealand where the landforms are ancient. It is, in fact, still an active volcanic area where outbursts of modest activity are not uncommon, but where more major eruptions may occur at any time. Rotorua forms one link in a chain of activity, running in a line from Mount Ruapehu in the south, through Taupo and Rotorua to White Island off the coast, and so on up to the Kermadec Islands as far as Tonga.

The 'thermal wonderland'

The Rotorua field of activity is the most extensive, and
though its once most widely publicised features, the Pink and
White Terraces, were destroyed in 1886 by the great Tarawera
eruption, it is still world renowned for its remaining wonders.

Perhaps most spectacular are the geysers, erupting columns of
scalding water some 25–30 m (80–100 ft) into the air. No less
amazing are the craters of boiling mud, pools of crystal-clear
boiling water, hissing fumaroles of sulphurous gas, and

The 'thermal wonderland'

glittering silica terraces, built up over centuries of nearby activity. Almost every colour of the rainbow can be found in either the multitude of thermal pools, surrounding rock formations, or soils.

Amazingly enough, still sited within all this activity is the village of Te Whakarewarewa, where locals enjoy and employ the thermal waters for heating, bathing and cooking, as their ancestors have done for generations.

Mount Tarawera

Though small by comparison with some of New Zealand's ancient volcanic explosions, the eruption of Mount Tarawera on 10 June 1886 was a devastating event. It resulted in considerable loss of life and the total destruction of a number of small settlements, including the well-established and important village of Te Wairoa.

The eruption was also unique in that the force of its action opened up a vast fissure of almost 16 km (10 miles) along the mountain's entire ridge, passing through each of its triple peaks and extending southwest as far as the present Waimangu, itself a remarkable thermal area today. From the three major peaks, Wahanga, Ruawahia and Tarawera, a violent curtain of fire was blasted out while at the same time masses of red-hot material were hurled some 30 km (18 miles) skywards before falling back onto the mountain's slopes and much of the surrounding country.

Mount Tarawera

Just to the southwest of the mountain, and at much the same time, another enormous explosion beneath Lake Rotomahana lifted a mass of semi-fluid muddy material perhaps as much as 10 km (6 miles) into the air. The force of the impact as the mass fell back to earth caused a wall of the same molten material to flow outwards as a violent tidal-wave for some 6 km (4 miles) in every direction and at speeds of perhaps 200 kph (124 mph), obliterating everything in its path. It was mud from this same explosion that also fell over a large area of the countryside, burying a number of settlements and destroying the extensive village of Te Wairoa.

Apart from 108 lives lost (including seven Europeans), the destruction of the Pink and White Terraces at Rotomahana was viewed by many as the major loss due to the eruption. Descriptions of these wonders abound, though most expressing their feelings describe themselves as being quite unable to ever

Ruins of Hiona (Zion) Church at Te Wairoa.

Mount Tarawera

do them justice. But lost they were, for where they had once existed on Rotomahana's shoreline there was now just a vast crater, which eventually filled with water, creating a new Lake Rotomahana many times larger than the original.

The terraces had brought a constant and growing stream of visitors to the area since the 1850s. They had also brought great prosperity to the village of Te Wairoa and its inhabitants, most of whom were involved in the fledgling tourism industry. Two hotels, a flour mill, three stores, a temperance hall, a school, church, a fine carved whare tupuna (meeting house) and many residences of both traditional Maori and European form attested to its growing importance.

Though totally destroyed by the eruption and abandoned by its survivors, the site of the village can still be visited and recognised today. A number of the original buried buildings have been excavated and a splendid museum devoted entirely to the eruption and its aftermath has been recently established.

The Pink and White Terraces

The Pink and White Terraces were the result of untold centuries of thermal activity, but in particular, the actions of two immense geysers known respectively as Otukapuarangi and Te Tarata. It was the siliceous content of the water cascading from these geysers that had, by precipitation, coated the underlying rocks as it flowed downwards, creating the terraces.

Both geysers stood on elevated sites close to the shoreline of the original Lake Rotomahana, which together with the nearby (but much smaller) Lake Rotomakariri, lay in a swampy depression, below and to the southwest of Mount Tarawera. Though only a fraction of the size of the present Rotomahana, it was that lake and its lake edge terraces that had brought it fame.

The larger White Terrace (Te Tarata) covered an area of some 2.8 ha (7 acres) and rose from the lake edge in a series of semi-

The White Terrace,
or Te Tarata.

The Pink and White Terraces

circular, nearly snow-white silica steps or basins, each a different height to the others and filled (as many claimed) with the most exquisite turquoise-blue water. The water temperature in each basin rose as they climbed towards Te Tarata Geyser, some 24 m (80 ft) above.

The Pink Terrace (Otukapuarangi) stood opposite the White Terrace and on the west shore of Rotomahana. Of a delicate salmon-pink colour, it was smaller in extent than the white, covering 1.4 ha (3 acres), and rising to a height of 18.2 m (60 ft). At the top its great geyser cauldron of some 15.2 m (50 ft) in diameter regularly overflowed, cascading its silica-rich waters downwards, constantly building up the formation.

Acclaimed often as the 'Eighth Wonder of the World', the Pink and White Terraces were completely destroyed during the eruption of Mount Tarawera, Lake Rotomahana today marking the extent of the crater left after the event.

Lake Taupo

A chain of volcanic activity still crosses the centre of the North Island and remnants of peaks and craters from past eruptions are abundant. Among these are many extinct, dormant and active volcanoes, some from the past undoubtedly numbering among the world's greatest explosions.

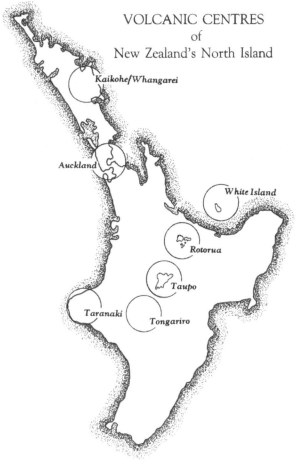

VOLCANIC CENTRES
of
New Zealand's North Island

Kaikohe/Whangarei

Auckland

White Island

Rotorua

Taupo

Taranaki

Tongariro

Lake Taupo

The North Island's largest lake, Lake Taupo, conceals a volcanic vent in its northeastern sector which erupted in AD 186, creating the world's largest such event during at least the past 5000 years. More than 30 cubic kilometres (7.2 cu miles) of volcanic material were erupted, spreading ash and pumice over some 30,000 square kilometres (11,600 sq miles). At the same time it spewed across the landscape — at a speed of probably 300 m (328 yards) per second — a scalding sea of ignimbrite that incinerated almost everything in its path, finally blanketing some 20,000 square kilometres (7700 sq miles) with a layer of rock and pumice that forms today's Taupo plateau.

However, that eruption was nothing compared to the one that created the caldera now filled by Lake Taupo. It happened 26,500 years ago and blew out some 600 cubic kilometres (144 cu miles) of material. It may well have been the greatest volcanic eruption ever.

White Island

White Island forms New Zealand's northernmost active volcano in the chain of thermal activity stretching from Ruapehu in the south, through Taupo and Rotorua to the central Bay of Plenty coastline. Lying almost 50 km (30 miles) offshore, it can be visited from Rotorua or Whakatane by helicopter, or by special vessels from Whakatane.

Visible from the mainland, White Island rises 321 m (1053 ft) above sea level and generally carries a plume of steam, gas and sometimes ash rising from its often violent crater, which itself lies some 70 m (229 ft) below sea level.

Known to Maori as Whakaari (possibly a reference to its

White Island

visible white cloud) the island received its more general name of White Island from Captain James Cook, who noted in his log for 1 November 1769: 'I have named it White Island because as such it always appeared to us.'

Attempts to establish an industry on the island by mining its sulphur deposits began in 1885 and continued intermittently until 1933. For a variety of reasons, however, none of these ventures was very successful, and one in particular proved a disaster. In February 1914 a new company began mining operations but in September of the same year a collapse of part of the crater rim sent a lahar across the crater floor, sweeping all before it into the sea. No trace of the buildings or any of the ten workers employed there remained.

To walk on the very floor of an active volcano, to experience the sounds, the smells, the brilliant colours, the trembling of the earth, and to look down into the seething crater itself, is an awesome adventure and is only undertaken with experienced guides and strict requirements.

Another remarkable feature of White Island are the colonies of Australasian gannets and grey-faced petrels that breed on its southern and western outer ridges. The gannets, numbering some 5000 breeding pairs, can often be seen, with folded wings, diving into the sea as they seek their food. The petrels, however, despite numbering perhaps as many as 60,000, are rarely seen because during the winter months, in particular, they spend only the nights ashore, arriving back at dusk or later and departing again for the open sea before daylight.

Rock, ice and water

Waikoropupu Springs

The remarkable geology of the Takaka Valley, in the Golden Bay area of the South Island, gives rise to Australasia's largest freshwater springs, known as Waikoropupu, or locally as Pupu Springs. Situated only about 2.5 km (one and a half miles)

Waikoropupu Springs

inland from the tidal reach of the Takaka River, the lake-like proportions of these amazing springs are supplied by a cluster of eight vents in the main basin, the largest of which is 1.5 m (5 feet) wide. There is one major vent and several smaller ones in the 'Dancing Sands' arm (illustrated on page 107) and others in an area known as the Fish Creek system. Together, these springs discharge an average 14,000 litres of water every second!

Though there are some 60 larger freshwater springs in other parts of the world, none provides water of equal clarity to that of Waikoropupu Springs. Visibility in the waters here is more than 60 m (200 ft) and a constant temperature of 11.7°C is maintained.

Together with the springs, the Takaka Valley can also claim the deepest and longest cave system in the southern hemisphere and it is this, together with its complex system of underground drainage, that provides the flow from Waikoropupu. While water can enter the underground cave system at many points, its geological make-up prevents any discharge except at Waikoropupu Springs and at least three offshore springs on the seabed of Golden Bay.

Glaciers

As an island nation, New Zealand has an amazing diversity of geographic features. Lying between latitude 29 degrees south and 52.5 degrees south, its some 700 assorted islands vary from subtropical to subantarctic. However, more than 98 percent of the country's land area is contained in its two major land masses, the North Island and the South Island.

Though the North Island has its high, snow-topped peaks and glaciers, the South Island is noted for them, particularly its Southern Alps. This chain of magnificent mountains extends almost the island's full length, reaching its highest point at the summit of Aoraki/Mount Cook, near the central part of the range. It is in this same area where some of the most noted of the South Island's 360 named glaciers are to be found. These

Glaciers

amazing flows of shattered, twisted and jumbled ice drain both east and west from the alps.

Those glaciers running east gradually descend to a final elevation of between 760 and 912 m (2500 and 3000 ft) and into the interior river catchments of the island. Those falling to the west flow directly out to the coast. Two of these latter, the Franz Josef and Fox, drop rapidly down into the thick rainforest and terminate only some 300 m (1000 ft) above sea level. They are among the world's largest temperate region glaciers, and their rate of descent places the Franz Josef, in particular, among the world's fastest flowing.

The Southern Alps themselves began as a build-up on the ocean floor some 100 to 200 million years ago, and were slowly pushed up with the land some time between 50 and ten million years ago.

That same period saw a succession of four ice advances, the last ending only about 10,000 years ago. It covered most of the alps, and Fiordland to the southwest, with vast glaciers and sheets of ice. Some of these incredible rivers of ice, up to 1824 m (6000 ft) deep, eventually ground their way east, creating the hollows now occupied by Manapouri, Te Anau, Wakatipu, Pukaki, Rotoroa and almost all the other main South Island lakes.

Those flowing west followed mountain valleys towards the coast. These ice flows were also so thick and powerful that they

Glaciers

gouged the valley floors and deepened them well below sea level. As the ice gradually retreated during the next 10,000 years, the sea moved in, creating the magnificent Milford and other southern fiords.

Aoraki/Mount Cook

New Zealand's highest mountain, Aoraki/Mount Cook, at 3754 m (12,316 ft), dominates the many spectacular valleys, glaciers and neighbouring peaks contained within the 70,000 ha (173,000 acre) Mount Cook National Park. First declared a national park in 1953, it received world heritage status as a natural area in 1986.

Encompassing part of the South Island's Southern Alps, the park contains 19 peaks more than 3000 m (9800 ft) high, innumerable glaciers, the longest of which, the Tasman, stretches for 28 km (17 miles), and vast valleys gouged out in past millennia by glaciers almost 2000 m (6000 ft) deep.

Aoraki/Mount Cook

The whole park area, noted as one of the world's finest training grounds for mountaineers, has the heaviest concentration of mountain ice anywhere. It was here that Sir Edmund Hillary, conqueror of Everest, honed many of his skills. The first ascent of Aoraki/Mount Cook itself was made on Christmas Day 1894 by George Graham, Jack Clarke and Tom Fyfe, a trio of amateurs who went on to become noted guides.

Mount Cook National Park, as part of the Southern Alps, has been subjected to immense geological movements, with the western edge of the Pacific Plate being crumpled by the Australian Plate to form the alps during the last five million years. The alps still continue to rise at some 5 mm ($\frac{1}{5}$ in) per year, which together with natural weathering and erosion can trigger some frightening movements. During December 1991 part of the summit of Aoraki/Mount Cook collapsed, sending an estimated 14 million cubic metres (493 million cu ft) of rock and rubble plunging down to the surface of the Tasman Glacier at speeds approaching 600 kph (370 mph). The result was a reduction of the mountain's height by 10 m (33 ft).

The Southern Alps were named as such by Captain James Cook while sailing along the west coast in 1770, during his first voyage to New Zealand. As a tribute to this great navigator his name was subsequently applied to the highest peak.

However, the mountain already had a name and featured in the legends of Ngai Tahu Maori of the South Island. They call the mountain Aoraki/Aorangi ('Cloud Piercer'), after the eldest son of Raki, the sky father. The same legends record that the

113

Aoraki/Mount Cook

South Island was once, in fact, a canoe belonging to Aoraki.
During a voyage it was stranded where it now lies. Aoraki and
his brothers (the crew) were forced to climb onto the high side of
the vessel above the waterline where they have remained ever
since. They ultimately became the peaks of the magnificent
Southern Alps, Aoraki himself being the tallest of them all.

Punakaiki Rocks

Some 30 million years ago, countless billions of microscopic marine creatures and plants, having expired, sank to the ocean floor, creating a distinct layer. Layer upon layer were subsequently laid down as the millennia passed, each, however, separated by a thinner band of gravelly material, often described as mudstone. Ultimately, the immense weight and pressure resulted in the layers of fossil material compounding into limestone, each still distinguished by the thin bands of mudstone.

Earth movements at some remote time lifted these deposits above sea level, where they have since been subjected to erosion. A heavy rainfall, combined with many centuries of wind-lashed

Punakaiki Rocks

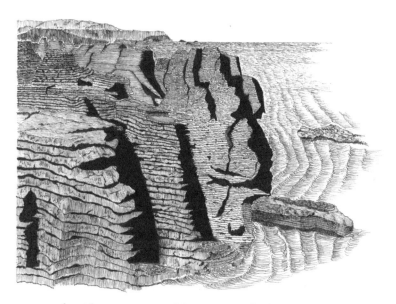

spray from heavy seas crashing against the base of the formations, has created a remarkable coastline feature. The same wave action has also created tunnels, surge chambers and blowholes along the waterline. Waves rushing into these cavities cause an explosive reaction, the sounds of heavy thunder, and a geyser-like ejection of water and spray high into the air.

The remarkable layered effect of these rocks has given rise to their often-used name of Pancake Rocks. They are, however, more properly known as Punakaiki, part of some 11 areas collectively known as the Punakaiki Reserves. They also form part of the Paparoa National Park, and are situated about midway between Westport and Greymouth.

Moeraki Boulders

These remarkable boulders occur on a stretch of beach known as Koekohe, on the east coast of the South Island. Lying south of Oamaru and between the communities of Hampden and Moeraki, they have provoked great interest for centuries.

The earliest European seafarers to see the boulders referred to them as the 'nine pins', believing them to have been either marbles or bowling balls belonging once to a race of giants.

They are, however, concretions or argillaceous limestone that were originally formed on the ocean floor at a time mudstone was accumulating, perhaps 60 million years ago. The boulders themselves may each have taken some five million years to create. Then, as the coastline rose, the boulders rose with it, and even now are being gradually eroded from the nearby cliffs, to lie on the beach itself. Some boulders, subjected to wild seas and centuries of exposure, have cracked apart, leaving only part of a shell, not unlike a discarded piece of orange peel.

Over the years, souvenir hunters have carried off most of the smaller boulders that once existed here. Now only those that are too heavy to move remain.

A Maori legend concerning the boulders' origins speaks of the wreck of one of the earliest canoes that arrived in this country from far-off Hawaiki, the nebulous homeland of New Zealand's Polynesians.

While travelling south on a quest for precious greenstone, and commanded by the explorer and navigator Hipo, the canoe *Te Arai-te-uru* was wrecked at a point named Matakaea, some

Moeraki Boulders

19 km (12 miles) south of Moeraki. A reef running seawards from Matakaea (now known as Shag Point) is said to be the petrified hull of *Te Arai-te-uru*, while Hipo himself remains, also petrified, in the form of a nearby prominent rock.

The Moeraki Boulders, lying still along the beach, represent the petrified remains of wreckage from the canoe in the form of eel baskets, calabashes and kumara.

Milford Sound and Mitre Peak

Milford Sound and Mitre Peak are almost synonymous. Milford Sound is probably the most magnificent fiord in the southern hemisphere, while Mitre Peak, named because of its resemblance to a bishop's mitre, or head-dress, rises spectacularly from the head of the fiord to a height of slightly more than 1695 m (5560 ft).

The waters of the sound, some 13 km (8 miles) long, were originally named Piopiotahi (after the native thrush) by Maori, as they searched the whole Fiordland coastline for precious greenstone. In fact, a reef of greenstone does exist above Anita Bay, near the entrance to the fiord where it meets the Tasman Sea. It was quarried for a time in 1842 to supply the Chinese market but was a short-lived venture. The name Milford Sound was apparently first applied to the fiord in 1823 by John Grono, a Welsh sealing captain, to commemorate the southern Welsh town of Milford Haven.

Milford Sound and Mitre Peak

All the fiords reaching the Tasman Sea, west of Fiordland's wild and mountainous main divide, were created during a sequence of ice ages, the last of these dating from about 70,000 to 10,000 years ago. It was a period when, on perhaps three or four occasions, great glaciers flowed down the main valleys, gouging the floors ever deeper, and honing back the mountains into sharp and serrated peaks. The size and weight of these massive glaciers ultimately ground the valley floors well below the present sea level. The walls themselves were left so sheer and high that they form the world's highest sea cliffs.

An incredible yearly Fiordland rainfall that can reach 10,000 mm (394 in) produces a unique environment for the area's marine life. Water cascading from surrounding mountains is stained by accumulated humus as it passes through the ancient beech forests and reaches the fiord, though pure, with the colour of weak tea. This darker fresh water creates a layer some 3 m (10 ft) thick, which sits on top of the warmer salt water, considerably filtering the sunlight.

The reduced light on the salt water suppresses the growth of seaweed, allowing an amazing variety of otherwise deepwater marine species (including a delicate black coral) to exist at only a tenth of the depth found elsewhere in the world.

A modern underwater observatory makes it possible to view in comfort the remarkable and undisturbed life of this marine community in its own environment.